MEASURING MANIA

MEASURING LENGTH

by Darice Bailer   illustrated by Kathleen Petelinsek

Published in the United States of America by Cherry Lake Publishing
Ann Arbor, Michigan
www.cherrylakepublishing.com

Consultants: Janice Bradley, PhD, Mathematically Connected Communities,
New Mexico State University; Marla Conn, ReadAbility, Inc.

Editorial direction: Red Line Editorial
Book design and illustration: The Design Lab

Photo credits: Nikolay Postnikov/Shutterstock Images, 4; Shutterstock Images, 5,
8, 18–19; Blend Images/Thinkstock, 6; First Class Photos/Shutterstock Images,
12; iStock/Thinkstock, 20

Library of Congress Cataloging-in-Publication Data
Bailer, Darice, author.
  Measuring length / by Darice Bailer.
       pages cm. — (Measuring mania)
  Audience: 5–8.
  Audience: K to grade 3.
  Includes bibliographical references and index.
  ISBN 978-1-62431-647-0 (hardcover) — ISBN 978-1-62431-674-6 (pbk.) —
ISBN 978-1-62431-701-9 (pdf) — ISBN 978-1-62431-728-6 (hosted ebook)
  1. Length measurement–Juvenile literature. I. Title.

  QC102.B25 2014
  530.8'1—dc23

                              2013029071

Cherry Lake Publishing would like to acknowledge
the work of The Partnership for 21st Century Skills.
Please visit www.p21.org for more information.

Printed in the United States of America
Corporate Graphics Inc.
January 2014

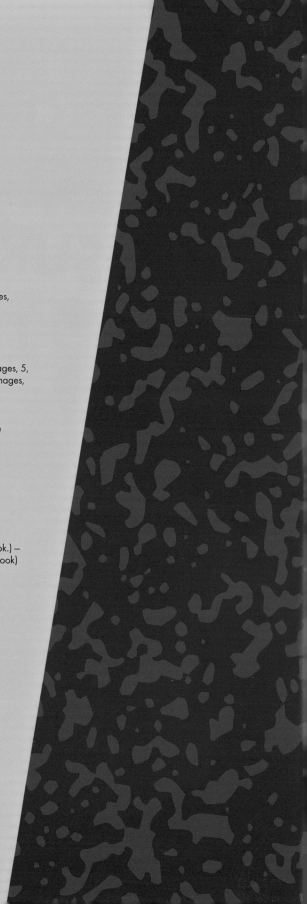

Table of Contents

CHAPTER ONE

What Is Length?

Measure the length of your favorite shoes.

You're growing! You need a new bike and new sneakers. But what size is right? You won't know if you don't measure!

Measuring tells you the **distance** from point to point. Measure the length of a worm end to end. See how tall your bike is from top to bottom. That's height. See how wide you can stretch your arms. That's width. Measure how far you run from place to place. That's distance.

How far can you run?

You can measure all these things. And you can see how much you've grown. Measuring gives you answers to all kinds of questions. Measuring helps you compare things. Let's measure length!

Have you grown since last year?

To do the activities in this book, you will need:

- ruler
- yardstick
- tape measure
- pencil
- paper

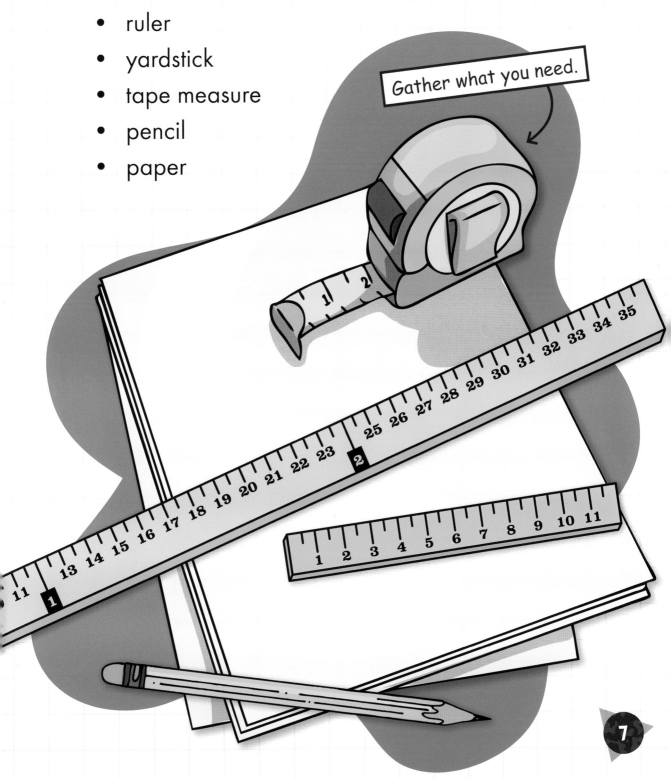

Gather what you need.

CHAPTER TWO

Starting Small

Use a ruler to measure small things.

What if you wanted to measure a small thing like your fingernail? What tool should you use? A **ruler** or a **yardstick**? A ruler measures small things like erasers, crayons, and books. A yardstick works better for longer things. It can measure the height of your bike or a grown-up.

A ruler has numbers on both sides. One side of the ruler counts from 1 to 12. This side is divided into **units** called inches. It can measure your finger in inches. There is a shorter way to write the word inch: in.

Measure photos, books, and school supplies with a ruler.

There are 12 inches on a ruler. Twelve inches equal one foot (0.3 meter). A ruler is one foot long. That is about the length of an adult foot. Three feet make one yard. Inches, feet, and yards are units in the **U.S. customary system**.

The ruler doesn't show 0 where it starts on the left or 12 where it ends on the right. Count the 12 inch-long spaces on the ruler.

Here is a chart showing units of length:
- 12 inches = 1 foot (0.3 m) (the length of a ruler)
- 3 feet = 1 yard (0.9 m) (three rulers = one yardstick)
- 1,760 yards = 1 mile (1,609 m)
- 5,280 feet = 1 mile (Phew! That's far!)

ACTIVITY

Go on a Scavenger Hunt!

INSTRUCTIONS:

1. Find a bug shorter than 1 inch.
2. Find a plant taller than 1 foot.
3. Find three things inside your house that are not the same width. (One must be a person!) Measure them. Which is the widest? Thinnest?
4. Find a toy about 1 foot long.
5. Find a piece of furniture more than 1 yard long.

To get a copy of this activity, visit www.cherrylakepublishing.com/activities.

What else can you find to measure?

CHAPTER THREE

Measuring Tools

How big around do you think the puppy's neck is?

Sophie's new puppy needs a collar. Sophie needs to measure her puppy's neck. Then she can get the right collar size.

Her friend Harry knows a ruler or yardstick would not work. He gets a **tape measure** instead.

The tape measure has different numbers on top and bottom. One side measures things in inches, feet, and yards. Harry and Sophie will use that side.

Tape measures are made of cloth, plastic, or metal.

Harry sees that the tape is 10 feet (3 m) long. That is as tall as his basketball hoop! Harry can measure very long or tall things with a tape measure. Harry wraps the tape around the puppy's neck. Now they know which size collar to buy.

Be gentle if you measure your pet!

Guess the Distance

Find a friend. Get out a yardstick and tape measure and see how far you can jump!

1. Guess how far both of you can jump in inches.
2. Put the yardstick down on the floor. It will be the starting line!
3. Your friend should line up behind the yardstick. Then, have your friend jump!
4. Roll out the tape measure. See how far your friend jumped in inches. Write down the number.
5. Your turn!
6. How close were you to your guesses? What is the difference between your guesses and your real jumps?

To get a copy of this activity, visit www.cherrylakepublishing.com/activities.

CHAPTER FOUR

Length, Width, Height

The puppy's carrier should not be too big or too small.

Sophie and Harry are excited about the new puppy. Sophie also needs a pet carrier. The puppy will go to the vet in it.

What size should they buy? They need to find out the carrier's length, width, and height. Sophie thinks a yardstick will help. A yardstick is three feet long.

Three rulers equal the length of one yardstick.

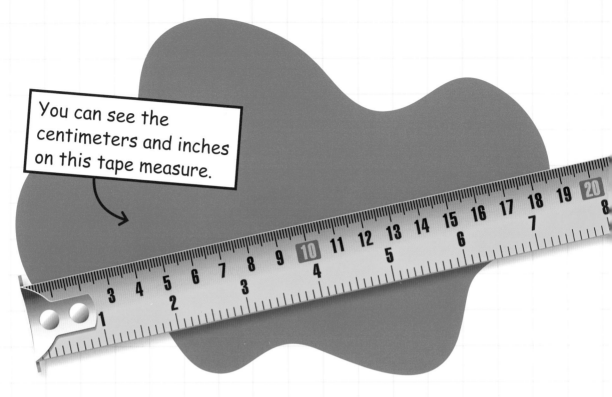

You can see the centimeters and inches on this tape measure.

Rulers, yardsticks, and tape measures have two sets of numbers. Sophie and Harry used inches and feet before. This time, they want to use the other numbers.

The other numbers are in the **metric system**. The metric system measures with units called centimeters and meters.

The metric system counts in tens. One hundred centimeters equal one meter. That is about 39 inches, or a little longer than a yard. There is a shorter way to write centimeters: cm.

Inches and Centimeters

INSTRUCTIONS:

1. **Height**

   Sophie thinks 36 inches is too tall for a carrier. They need one 12 inches shorter. How many inches do they need?

   How many feet is that?

   Look on a yardstick or tape measure. How many centimeters are in that many feet?

2. **Width**

   They need a carrier at least 1 foot wide. How many centimeters are in 1 foot?

3. **Length**

   The carrier should be half a yard from front to back. How many inches is half a yard?

   Now look on a yardstick or tape measure. How many centimeters is this?

To get a copy of this activity, visit www.cherrylakepublishing.com/activities.

Measuring Mania

The next time you ride your bike or walk somewhere, measure the distance.

What can you do with a ruler, a yardstick, and a tape measure? Like Harry and Sophie, you can measure all sorts of things. And you can measure in different ways!

Here are more fun ways to measure:

- Measure the width of your hand in inches and centimeters. Then measure a friend's hand. Whose is bigger?

- Pluck two blades of grass. How much taller is one than the other?

- What would you use to measure your waist? A ruler, a yardstick, or a tape measure? Measure your waist in inches and centimeters.

- What if you wanted to measure across the school playground? Do you think a tape measure would be long enough?

- You ride your bike or walk to a friend's house and want to know the distance. Ask a family member to drive it. The car **odometer** will tell you the distance. This tool measures how far you drive. There are even odometers for bikes!

Glossary

distance (DIS-tuhns) the length between two places

metric system (MEH-trik SIS-tum) a way to measure things based on the number ten using units such as centimeters and meters

odometer (oh-DAH-meh-tur) a tool that measures the distance you ride in a car or on a bike

ruler (ROO-lur) a long piece of plastic, wood, or metal that measures inches or centimeters

tape measure (TAYP MEZH-ur) a long piece of fabric or metal that unrolls to measure long things

units (YOO-nits) standard amounts that are used to measure things

U.S. customary system (YOO-es KUS-tuh-mer-ee SIS-tum) units of measurement typically used in the United States such as cups, quarts, miles, feet, and inches

yardstick (YAHRD-stik) a thin, long tool 36 inches long used for measuring

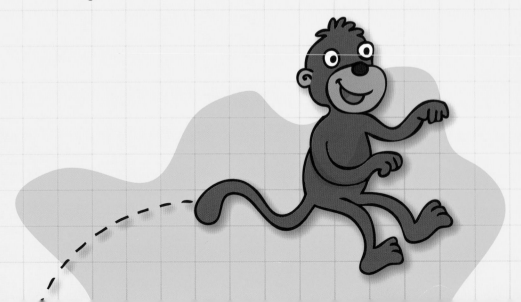

For More Information

BOOKS

Robbins, Ken. *For Good Measure: The Ways We Say How Much, How Far, How Heavy, How Big, How Old*. New York: Roaring Brook Press, 2010.

Schwartz, David M. *Millions to Measure*. New York: HarperCollins Publishers, 2003.

WEB SITES

Adapted Mind: Customary Distance— Choose the Best Estimate
http://www.adaptedmind.com/p.php?tagId=1051
Estimate the length of different things, including a whale or a horse. See if you're right!

Customary Units of Length: Word Problems
http://www.ixl.com/math/grade-2 /customary-units-of-length-word-problems
How much longer is one thing than another? Go figure!

Measure It Measurement Game
http://www.funbrain.com/measure/
You will find lots of fun games here. How long is the line in inches and centimeters? Look on the ruler and see!

Index

About the Author

Darice Bailer learned how to measure in Rochester, New York. As a kid she tried to build a tree house. She grew up to write many books for young kids. She became a journalist, too. Her stories have appeared in the *New York Times*. She lives in Connecticut with her husband.